Roaming the Northern Rails

Eric Treacy

Roaming the Northern Rails

PRC

This title first published 1976 by Ian Allan

This edition produced 1994 by
The Promotional Reprint Company Limited
exclusively for Bookmart Limited, Desford Road,
Enderby, Leicester LE9 5AD

ISBN 1 85648 177 8

Printed in China

CONTENTS

INTRODUCTION

PHOTOGRAPHIC AUTOBIOGRAPHY

I cast my mind back over forty-five years at which time I was not a small boy with ambitions to be an engine driver. I was in my early 20s, and looking for a hobby.

My work, running a large boys' club in the Liverpool Dockside made impossible the violent exercise on the Rugger field to which I had been accustomed. Instead, I was refereeing, or cheering on my lads' team in an abominable game played with a round ball! Golf was far too expensive for my limited financial resources, so I turned my attention to photography. I bust myself acquiring a Leica, a step I never regretted.

I soon found, however, that to give any satisfaction, photography must be directed to a purpose, otherwise one becomes just an aimless snapshotter, accumulating over the years a vast collection of unrelated snapshots which eventually end up on a bonfire.

Some there be who photograph pew ends, cathedrals and abbeys, birds and wild life; you name it, and there is some photographer who specialises in it. One day when I was wondering in which direction I should point my camera, I was meeting a train in Lime Street station when, suddenly, it hit me.* There, under that arched roof, with smoke and steam drifting in varied patterns, shadowy figures moving about, and at the centre of it all, the steam engine. There they stood, hissing, simmering, smoking; little ones, big ones, red ones and black ones. I knew immediately that here was a scene of infinite photographic possibilities, with an atmosphere which could better be captured by a painter than a photographer, but some of which one might succeed in conveying through the lens of a camera.

*Not the train!

Frontispiece: A3 Pacific No 4472 *Flying Scotsman* in steam at Steamtown, Carnforth.

This was my introduction to a hobby that I could pursue at odd moments: in lunch hours, on journeyings and a hobby with personal attachments.

The Railway consists of people as well as machines; on every footplate were a couple of men: in every signalbox were men ringing bells and pulling levers: on every mile of main railway line there were four good men and true looking after the track. And it was amongst such men that I numbered, during the last forty-five years many very good friends, and my happiest memories of pottering about railways consist of my contacts with railwaymen. I can't answer for other walks of life, but the railway world produces an astonishing variety of characters. I recall the courteous hospitality that I have experienced on footplates, in signalboxes and gangers' 'bothies' all over the British Isles. I recall the spirit that the old locomotive sheds generated; in spite of the dirt and mess which were inevitable, these sheds were places that had their own mystique, and even mythology. They had their characters: men who had done doughty deeds; men who were known as 'good enginemen'; there was the aristocracy of the 'top link'. Men who were proud of their sheds although they would not often admit it. The areas round the sheds were tight little communities in which the blue overalls were a uniform that men were proud to wear.

Do I exaggerate? I don't think so. I can remember clearly all these things in Wavertree in the 1930s as they were at the Edge Hill sheds.

In those days before 1939, my wife and I used to take our holidays in the Lake District. Occasionally I was allowed to borrow my father-in-law's car: but usually we would go by train and I would take my push bike in the guard's van. We stayed in Ullswater at a small hamlet called Howtown. Ullswater is a lovely lake with the added advantage that it is the nearest of the lakes to the West Coast main line. With an enormous reflex camera in the basket strapped to the handlebars, I would set off, one day for Penrith; another for Shap. It amazes me now, in old age, when I realise the distances I pedalled in high summer with that 'tonnage' in the front of the old bike.

There was a very kind photographer in Penrith called Tunley who used to allow me to use his darkroom for loading plates into my dark slides. In those days of plate cameras there were the problems of weight, and reloading. Often the only place to change plates was under the bedclothes in the hotel bedroom. There you struggled in pitch darkness getting hotter and hotter, sometimes mixing the fresh plates with the new ones, and occasionally leaving small chippings of glass between the sheets. Photography in those days could be a wearisome business: how different today when you can take enough film for a hundred exposures in your pocket and have no problems of reloading. Plates were horribly liable to crops of pin-holes, which were usually most prominent on one's best exposures, and defied all efforts at retouching.

Except for holidays in those days before 1939, I didn't get far from Merseyside. My photographic activities were confined to about 15 minutes in the morning, and about the same in the evening, weather and parochial engagements permitting. It was a matter of minutes to nip down on my bicycle from my vicarage to Edge Hill or Wavertree. Inevitably there was a certain local similarity in my photographic output! Camden Pacifics worked into Liverpool: it wasn't till after the war that Edge Hill received its own allocation of Pacifics. Far and away the best photographic location was in the Lime Street cutting, which I describe elsewhere in this book.

As I said earlier in this introduction, I started not with a Box Brownie but with a Leica. No camera looks better, feels better or performs better within its field. In its more recent forms it has become bulbous, even corpulent, and can scarce be thought of as a 'miniature' camera. The fact that I graduated from the Leica to something bigger is more a condemnation of me than the camera.

I lacked the facilities and the skill to process the small negatives in such a way as to produce good results. Study of the experts in this field of photography led me to the conclusion that a quarter plate reflex or press camera was the answer. There were times on a hot summer's day when I regretted my conversion, as I lugged a thing the size of a piano-accordion up some fly-infested railway embankment.

To jump several years, in the 1960s I turned entirely to film cameras. A Rolleiflex and a Super Ikonta fulfilled all my needs. The lens performance of both cameras is superb: modern films combine speed and lack of grain supremely well. I must confess that I still have a Leica which I use for colour work in the mountains.

Now, to return to those pre-war days. They were exciting days on the railways. There was colour and variety, and the excitement of competition between the four major companies. There was Mallard's 126mph between Stoke Tunnel and Peterborough. The trial runs of the LMS and LNER streamlined Pacifics. The story has it that the LMS speed trial from Euston to Crewe nearly ended in disaster as the train hit the cross-overs at Crewe at a speed of 60mph. For those who had the free time, these days were a photographer's joy, but not for me. I read about these great exploits of steam but did not see them.

I had one unforgettable holiday when I walked the track from Tebay to Carlisle, bed and breakfasting at cottages and farms each night. Thus, I missed nothing. I spent my time sitting on country stations, now closed, drinking tea in signal boxes, eating my sandwiches in gangers' huts. It was a privilege to meet and talk with these men, all of them countrymen. I learned much from them of the natural history and folk lore of the region. But the clouds of war were gathering — Munich in 1938; war in 1939. I joined the army and for five and a half years I was a wanderer on the face of the earth. My contacts with the railway were very few. Occasionally one of my Edge Hill driver friends would insist on my travelling on the footplate when I was going home on leave. I carried a small pocket camera with me wherever I went — strictly against regulations — but it was used more for regimental portraiture than for railways. There were times, however, when the regiment was billeted in the vicinity of a railway line and I was able to add a few unusual specimens to my collection.

When I was released in 1945 we went to live in the West Riding of Yorkshire at Keighley. Here was a vastly different scene from Merseyside. The old Midland line from Leeds to Carlisle threaded the Aire Valley just below where we lived. The newly rebuilt 'Royal Scots' and 'Jubilees' dominated the line with the Anglo-Scottish traffic. As I got my bearings in this new part of England, I discovered that I was only a shade over two hours travel by car from Shap Fell and that, even nearer at hand, there was the line from Settle to Ais Gill.

On such days — oft as I could manage, I would head north to one or other of these places. There was not as much traffic on the 'Long Drag' to Ais Gill, but the setting was superb. The line threads Ribblesdale, the wildest of all the Yorkshire Dales, climbing all the way. Pen-y-Ghent and Ingleborough stand as great sentinels in this open moorland; on the fairest days there is always plenty of wind, and rare is the day when you do not get a soaking. Through the gorge at Stainforth, past Horton-in-Ribblesdale, up to Ribblehead, the trains labour, before crossing the magnificent viaduct at Bally Moss and then plunging into Blea Moor tunnel. Across the viaducts at Dent Head and Arten Gill, through Dent station (about four miles from the village from which it takes its name), thence to Ais Gill, when they dive down the hill to Kirkby Stephen and Appleby. What a line! I had my first postwar footplate trip over this section on the down 'Thames-Clyde Express', the engine was a rebuilt 'Scot' No 6117 *Welsh Guardsman* in spotless condition. I will spare the reader the technical details of the journey: suffice to say that we were ten minutes late away from Leeds, and only two minutes late into Carlisle — and we lost those two minutes standing at signals outside Carlisle Citadel station!

I have covered hundreds of miles on the footplate, accompanied Kingmoor men from Euston to Carlisle on the Royal Scot: Neville Hill men from Leeds to Newcastle on the North Briton: Grantham men on the Heart of Midlothian from Newcastle to York: Holbeck men from Leeds to Carlisle on the Thames-Clyde and Waverley expresses: and Copley Hill men from Leeds to Kings Cross on the Yorkshire Pullman. Often I have taken my turn with the shovel, and gone into the tender to push the coal forward when occasion demanded. Engine drivers are a breed apart: years of responsibility have left their mark on them: responsibility not only for their engines and the passengers behind them, but for the training of their firemen. Any passenger on the footplate is there by courtesy of the driver, permit notwithstanding, and he does well to conduct himself accordingly. I suspect that engine crews appreciate the presence of a passenger who understands what the job is about, and who is familiar with what goes on 'up front'.

There is no doubt that good exhaust makes all the difference to a railway photograph, and I have to plead guilty to arranging some of my smoke effects. These were in days before atmospheric pollution had become the issue that it is today. I would tell the fireman precisely where I was going to be and then see what happened. Very rarely was I disappointed.

In 1949 I became an archdeacon. Now, never mind what an Archdeacon is, or does. In the old days when Anglican dignitaries dressed properly, he wore gaiters, which were most uncomfortable, but which marked him out as an ecclesiastically top person! Not 'as top' as a Bishop or a Dean but 'toppish'. As an Archdeacon I was an ex-officio member of a body called the Church Assembly which met three times a year in London, the meetings lasting for the inside of a week.

In the mornings and evenings of these weeks in London I would slip away to one of the London termini with my camera, thus covering an area previously closed to me. Harry Turrill the station master at Euston would often accompany me up Camden Bank — top hat an' all. This gave me a standing which I lacked at Kings Cross where the then station master, who shall remain nameless, was not so co-operative. However, I escaped his attentions in the area between the Gas Works and the Copenhagen Tunnels where the signalmen were most welcoming. The Top Shed at Kings Cross and Camden Shed were also happy hunting grounds.

I managed to combine reasonable attention to the Central Councils of the Church with my visits to the railways in London. When, sometimes, I crept into my seat in Church House,Westminster, a bit late and somewhat dishevelled, there were many who suspected what I had been up to but I don't think that the then Archbishop of Canterbury, Geoffrey Fisher, was aware that a 'Venerable' gentleman had been shinning up a signal post before reporting for duty. For those who don't know, 'Venerable' is the extraordinary title that the Church of England bestows upon Archdeacons!

And so the years passed and so did steam, but before it finally disappeared from the scene, I hunted it on Beattock, at Cockburnspath on the East Coast Route at York, Leeds, Newcastle and Edinburgh.

York is the Ecclesiastical HQ in the North, which meant that, as in London, I could combine attention to communications, vertical and horizontal. Around 1·00pm in York there is a lot happening. Lawrence Reeve and Geoffrey Bird — shed masters at York were always very hospitable.

I would often take my lunch break in Leeds, it being but twenty minutes from Wakefield. That accounts for the large numbers of photographs of trains leaving Leeds City and Central stations bearing my name.

My many years association with railways have brought me immense pleasure and blessed me with many friends, some of whom are, alas, now departed this life, and most of whom are retired from railway service. It would be impossible to mention them all, but one I would mention in particular, Ronnie Taylor, District Motive Power Superintendent at Leeds, now retired, who opened all doors at Holbeck for me, and who in the last days of steam on the Settle-Carlisle line accompanied me himself on the footplate of a 'Britannia' to Carlisle. He drove most of the way, and I fired, but being a Doncaster man he did not think too highly of our 'Britannia'.

How conservative these railwaymen are! Unfortunately a Doncaster built A3 had failed the previous day with a hot box.!

Three things will live long in my memory. The first was when a 'Black Five' No 5428 was named *Eric Treacy* at Tyseley. The christening was performed by an old friend of mine and a railway enthusiast, Leonard Wilson, Bishop of Birmingham. His bearded face will be remembered by many who saw him conduct the Annual Festival of Remembrance organised by the British Legion at the Albert Hall. He was famous for his bravery in a Japanese PoW camp after he had been taken prisoner when he was Bishop of Singapore. This naming was a very kind thought on the part of Brian Hollingsworth and Geoffrey Drury, the joint owners of the locomotive.

The second was when I was invited to open the Lakeside and Haverthwaite Railway in 1973. It was somewhat overshadowed by the fact that the Duchess of Kent had opened the North Yorkshire Moors Railway the day before. The occasion was marked by a gargantuan lunch at Lakeside at which we were the guests of 'Sealink'. I cut the tape at Lakeside and down the bank we went to Haverthwaite, stopping at Newby Bridge to plant a commemorative tree. A very good time was had by all and by none more than my wife and myself.

The third thing which has given me great pleasure is my election as President of the Keighley & Worth Valley Railway. It is a privilege to be associated with a body of such enthusiasts. I think that I can safely claim that it has a greater variety of motive power than any other preserved railway. Its first chairman was Mr R. M. Cryer, now MP for Keighley, and it is largely due to his initiative that the Worth Valley line owes its existence. I do my best not to be a nominal President, but the duties of a diocesan bishop are such that my visits are spasmodic, but whenever I go I am impressed by the sustained enthusiasm of the members. It may be a dangerous thing to say, but I think that there are more people who go to Haworth to visit the railway than to visit the Brontë shrine at the top of the hill!

One of the things that I have always valued in the course of my railway 'doings' is my association with the House of Ian Allan. It started in the late 1940s when Ian was leaving the employment of the Southern Railway and launching out into publishing. I was one of the first of the railway photographic fraternity to send my work to him. In 1948 he published my first book 'Steam Up'. Since then his firm has published four other of my books, and this will be the sixth. His has been a success story: his firm has published books covering a wide field, has its own printing works, operates a travel agency and is in the hotel business. I take pleasure in the knowledge that I have been with him since the beginning and I cherish the hope that in his early days in railway publishing I was of some help to him. He has played no small part in creating public interest in railways; even if he has bred a race of spotters who, at times, have been a confounded nuisance!

The intention of this book is to cover the period of transition from steam to diesel electric, and on to electric traction. In a number of instances, I have depicted the new forms of motive power in the old and familiar settings.

The world of railway photography has experienced a revival in the last few years. When steam disappeared from our railways, there were many who put their cameras away and decided that no longer was there anything worth photographing. Gradually, however, they have woken up to the fact that there are photographic possibilities about the diesel. In a sense, every diesel or electric engine looks the same, but this is not true of the setting or the lighting. Of course, some of these new locomotives are better than others. 'Deltics' are fine, powerful machines, and they look good, but they do not give the impression of *working* as did a steam engine.

That, I think, is the chief thing that is lacking with the new forms of motive power. They don't communicate in the way that a steam engine did. A run-down 'Black Five' clambering up Shap from the south, clouds of black smoke shooting skyward, the bark from the chimney getting slower and slower as the hill steepened, seemed to be saying "this hill is absolute hell, but I think I can just make it". As it passed you, you could almost feel the exhaustion of the engine.

Not so a diesel or an electric. Steadily it races to the top with effortless superiority. You don't feel sorry for it: you don't feel anything at all, except a sneaking admiration for its mechanical efficiency. Its passing is a non-event, whereas the passing of a steam engine was always an event. It advertised its coming and you could prepare for a 'grand entry' whereas these modern things are upon you and past you before you have time to realise what has happened.

I was told the other day that chalked inside the cab of a diesel locomotive was the message: "Come back steam. All is forgiven." I suppose that there remain a number of loco men who were brought up in steam, and who have never really taken to anything else. They will tell you that a steam engine possessed a personality. In every shed there were steam engines that were popular, and others that the men hated. Some wouldn't steam whatever you did to them; some were so rough that they shook their crews to pieces; some had a jinx on them so that something would always go wrong with them when it was important that everything should go right, whereas others were favourites with the men; engines that could be trusted, that steamed freely on a bag of chips — and it wasn't just a matter of maintenance but could only be put down to that strange perversity of inanimate matter whereby two machines made of the same material in the same place and built from the same engineer's drawings could behave in entirely different ways.

In days of steam, between drivers and their engines there existed an almost personal relationship. Sometimes, it was more hate than love but there was a relationship and I believe that it consisted of a number of things; in the first place the steam engine was basically a simple piece of machinery, and could be understood, which is more than can be said about the more modern forms of motive power. In the second place, the driver drove his engine and was not just at the mercy of a complicated box of tricks, therefore, he could humour his engine and could master its moods. Before setting out on his journey, the driver went round his engine giving it those final touches which would ensure a good performance.

And I am sure of something else. Some of those second-men in the diesels who are getting plumper than is good for them could do with a spell with the shovel!

There are many who are sad at the passing of the steam age. Is it only, I wonder, the steam engine for which they mourn, or is it the more personal age of which the steam engine was part? Electronics and the computer are taking over; speed is the master, and in such a situation personal contacts between railwaymen and the public are not impossible but more difficult to achieve.

The pictures in this book cover an area in the British Isles roughly north of a line from North Wales to Humberside. Neither my finances nor my time have premitted my exploring areas in the South of England, with the exception of the London area. For holidays we have always set our compass on a northward bearing. I am a Southerner by birth, but since 1929 I have lived in the North, and I have loved every minute of it. It is a bracing and stimulating place in which to live, the people are grand and the countryside superb. The railways have played an important part in the industrial development of the area, they have carted the coal away from the pits, and have fed the mills and factories with raw materials, and carried their products to the ports; they have penetrated the valleys, breasted the hills; they have brought prosperity to small communities which, otherwise, would have wasted away. The railway has played a tremendous part in the social development of the North during the last 150 years, and now lines have been closed, the track removed, and the juggernauts of the road have taken over — and — the safest form of transport has given place to the most dangerous, measured in terms of human lives.

Progress? This present age has curious ideas of progress, but I suppose that is to be expected when the accountants call the tune. The modern question is not "is it needed?" but "does it pay?"

The photographs in this book are a salute to the steam which has departed — and a muted welcome to the forms of traction which have replaced it.

COUNTY OF LANCASTER

I spent ten years before the 1939-45 war in Liverpool. At the end of the war when I was released from the Army, there was no parish in Liverpool hanging out its flags for me, so I took myself over the Pennines to Yorkshire. Thirty years in the West Riding have done nothing to lessen my love for Merseyside. Not surprising really, for it was in Liverpool that I met my wife, was ordained to the ministry, and had my first parish.

Of course Lancashire is more than Merseyside — but I am afraid that my railway peregrinations were mostly in the area from Lime Street to Wavertree, for the obvious reason that here the line literally threaded my parish. So it was, that, greatly daring, I penetrated the short tunnels at Edge Hill in to the Lime Street cutting, surely one of the most exciting locations anywhere in Britain.

The arches across the cutting gave a cathedral-like impression, creating wonderful patterns of light and shade. A mile or so down the cutting you could hear the locomotive getting hold of its train as it left Lime Street Station and hit the foot of the bank, soon you could see a vast cloud of exhaust shooting up in to the arches and then slowly out of that sulphurous fog would emerge the blunt nose of the locomotive: thus would the "Merseyside Express" plough up the hill — the noise deafening — the whole spectacle so breath-taking that you might well forget to release the shutter.

This cutting was a dangerous place. Not, as you might think, on account of the trains, but because of the various missiles thrown into the cutting by the denizens of Edge Hill; it was not unknown for old bicycles, bedsteads, pots and pans to land on the track and the P.W. men between Edge Hill and Lime Street had a strong case for danger money. Now in 1975 the cutting is no place for the likes of me, electrics tear up and down the hill: it is all so silent: there are no up and down tracks, there is what is called "permissive running" so that trains go up where they used to go down, and vice versa.

Sometimes I would park my push bike in the guard's van and venture in an easterly direction to the Euston-Glasgow main line, where one could hunt the "Coronation Scot", but the flat lands of mid-Lancashire — in my opinion — failed to produce the atmosphere and excitement of the Liverpool area. Not only that, I had a host of friends in signal boxes, and at Edge Hill sheds, who kept me informed of anything exciting that was about to happen, as, for instance, when the first "Duchess" Pacific worked into Lime Street from Crewe. What a sight that was. Those were good days — but the storm clouds of war were gathering, and soon life was to change for all of us. And for me — the Army.

"Nobbut just" in Lancashire is a place called Carnforth, and adjoining Carnforth Station, "Steamtown". There you will find Dr Peter Beet, aided and abetted by Joe Greenwood, cherishing a superb collection of locomotives, including, at the time of writing, a German Pacific, an S.N.C.F. Nord Pacific, *Flying Scotsman*, *Pendennis Castle*, *Green Arrow*, a couple of Stanier Class 5s, and a lot more.

Carnforth MP Depot and its layout of tracks have been taken over as they stood, including everything that one associates with a running shed. In addition to the actual engine shed, there is a turntable, water cranes, coaling stage, and ash disposal tower.

Below: Liverpool to London express at Edge Hill, "Jubilee" 3 cyl 4-6-0 No 5624 *St Helena*

Right: Up "Merseyside Express" in Lime Street Cutting. Rebuilt Scot No 46124 *London Scottish*

Left and below left: Changing scene at Liverpool Lime Street. Upper; Electric locomotive E3185. Lower; Rebuilt "Scot" No 46144 *Honourable Artillery Company* — both on trains for Euston.

Below: Up "Merseyside Express" at Edge Hill "Princess" Pacific No 46207 *Princess Arthur of Connaught*

Below left: Scene at the coaling stage at Edge Hill Motive Power Depot

Right and below right: Two scenes at Steamtown, Carnforth.

Left: "Crab" 2-6-0 No 2876 at Farington with Express freight train.

Below left: Manchester to Glasgow train at Preston "Patriot" class No 5544.

Below: Barrow to Euston train leaves Lancaster. "Jubilee" 3 cyl 4-6-0 No 45687 *Neptune*

Left: Liverpool to Holyhead train at Edge Hill. 2-6-0 No 2951 piloting ex LNWR 4-4-0 *Coronation.*

Below left: Brush class 47 diesel-electric locomotive in Lime Street station, Liverpool.

Below: *Turbomotive* No 6202 at Wavertree with the up "Merseyside Express".

Above: EMI Bo-Bo No 27004 leaves Manchester, London Road with train for Harwich.

Below: Preston to Manchester stopping train at Buxton. Hughes 4-6-0 No 10412.

CUMBRIA: WESTMORLAND

Just north of Carnforth is the boundary with what was once the county of Westmorland, but which is now, thanks to local government reorganisation the new county of Cumbria. Travelling north by rail there was always a feeling that you had escaped from the prison of industry and the squalor that accompanies it: there were the stone walls up the fell sides; there were becks of crystal clear water tumbling down the hills — and there were sheep, thousands of them, cropping the turf.

To the west of Oxenholme are the hills of Lakeland, with the Langdale Pikes easily recognisable. In steam days engines worked hard up the hill to Grayrigg, then eased off through the Lune Valley. Over the water splash at Dillicar troughs, through Tebay, an ugly little railway town at the foot of Shap Bank. Then the hard work started — 1 in 75 all the way to the top, and the driver hoping against hope that he would not be stopped half way up at Scout Green. When this happened, there could be trouble in restarting, especially if there were a wet rail.

Then, on to one of the best known bits of line in England, past Shap Wells to the Summit. A place where the winds blow, and the clouds gather, even in the summer, to unload themselves on the just and the unjust. A place where those who liked bird watching could find much to interest them, and where curlews pipe their melodious song. Forty five years ago when I first found my way on to Shap Fell, I could guarantee solitude, I had it all to myself except for the sheep and the curlews. In the latter days of steam, the place was haunted by enthusiasts with tape recorders and cameras. Who could blame them? It was a sight to stir the heart — a "Duchess" or a "Princess" blasting its way up the hill with a train of 400 tons behind it. Exhaust shooting up into the sky, a deafening roar from the chimney, and all in slow motion as the train passed at no more than 25 or 30 miles per hour.

And of one thing you could be sure, out of a cloudless blue sky, a cloud would appear over the sun at the crucial moment — only to disappear immediately the train had passed.

Then, over the top, and down the hill, through Shap, past Harrison's belching lime works, through the woods at Thrimby, round the bend at Clifton, and so to Penrith, just over the Cumberland border. I have spent many holidays on Shap and studied locomotive form without coming to any conclusions as to locomotive performance. I would see a Pacific making an awful fuss with a light train, and a Black 5 cantering up the hill unassisted with 350 tons behind the tender; some engines blackening the sky with smoke, others with but a whisp of exhaust from their chimneys. I suppose it all had to do with such things as the way drivers handled their engines, the condition of the engine, the quality of the coal and the state of the fire. It mattered not to the spectator to whom it was all fascinating in its variety and unexpectedness. To see an electric scudding up the hill nowadays at 80 miles per hour is fantastic: but when you have seen one, you have seen the lot.

I hate to say it, but the engine that appeared to me to be the least bothered by the hill was a Bulleid "Merchant Navy" (35017 *Belgian Marine*) during the locomotive exchanges in 1948. In a pouring rain storm it trotted up the bank with the "Royal Scot" as if on the flat.

Left: Winter's day on Shap. View from footplate of Stanier Pacific No 46257 *City of Salford* on the up "Caledonian" at Thrimby Grange.

Above: Up "Mid-day Scot" at Low Gill. Pacific No 46221 *Queen Elizabeth*

Below: English Electric Type 4 diesel-electric on the up "Mid-day Scot" in the Lune Valley at Tebay.

Three views at Penrith.

Right: "Royal Scot" No 6135 *East Lancs Regt* leaves Penrith with Perth to Euston train.

Far right: Evening train from Perth to the South leaves Penrith

Below right: Class 2P, 4-4-0 No 652 pilots "Jubilee" 4-6-0 on Glasgow to Liverpool and Manchester train.

Above left: Keswick portion of the up "Lakes Express" leaves Penrith behind "Precursor" tank No 6824.

Left: Up "'Mid-day Scot" takes water at the Dillicar troughs, Tebay. "Princess" Pacific No 46209 *Princess Beatrice*

Above: Up "Mid-day Scot" at Low Gill. Rebuilt "Scot" No 46148 *Manchester Regiment.*

Left: Two English-Electric class 50 diesel-electrics nearing Shap summit with the Birmingham Scotsman.

Below left: Under a stormy sky, up "Mid-day Scot" at Clifton, on the northern approach to Shap. "Princess" Pacific No 6201 *Princess Elizabeth*

Left: Ex LNWR G Class 0-8-0 No 59155 at Shap Wells with freight train.

Below left: Stanier Pacific No 46238 *City of Carlisle* at Strickland with Perth to London train.

Below: "Jubilee" 3 cyl 4-6-0 No 45719 *Glorious* at Shap Village with Glasgow to Manchester train.

Left: English Electric type 4 diesel-electric at Shap Wells with down "Royal Scot"

Below left: Stanier "Black 5" No 44735 pilots "Duchess" Pacific up Shap with Birmingham to Glasgow train.

Below: Carlisle to London train halts at Shap station. Rebuilt "Scot" No 6101 *Royal Scots Greys*

Right: Glasgow to Manchester train passes Harrison's Lime Works. "Jubilee" 3 cyl 4-6-0 No 45671 *Prince Rupert*.

41

Left: English Electric Class 50 Diesel-Electric No 408 at Shap Wells with down "Royal Scot".

Below left: Stanier Pacific No 46231 *Duchess of Atholl* at Shap Wells with Birmingham-Glasgow train.

Below: Glasgow to Manchester train passes Shap station. "Jubilee" 3 cyl 4-6-0 No 45661 *Vernon*

Far left: Freight train in the woods at Great Strickland. Stanier 2 cyl 4-6-0 No 45140.

Far left below: Class 4MT 2-6-4T climbs Shap under a stormy sky with Oxenholme to Carlisle train.

Left: Carlisle to Preston train leaves Penrith. Class 4P 3 cyl Compound 4-4-0 No 1101.

Below: Class 2P 4-4-0 No 40694 pilots "Britannia" Pacific No 70050 *Firth of Clyde* at Clifton with Glasgow to Liverpool and Manchester train.

CUMBRIA: CUMBERLAND

Right: Pair of English-Electric Class 50 diesel-electric locomotives leave Carlisle Citadel with Glasgow train.

From Penrith to Gretna it was Cumberland, with Carlisle as the focal point. With Shap behind, north bound trains were taking it easy into Carlisle; with Shap ahead, south bound trains were building up a good head of steam for the climb, albeit an easy one compared with that from the South.

In the Eden Valley, buildings were of the warm red sandstone of the area; in ploughing time, the earth was a dark red. To the west of Penrith the sharp edges of Saddleback are visible, and to the East, the Pennines begin to subside into the gap threaded by Hadrian's Wall as they reach the Border. This is gentle pastoral country in which there is more arable than sheep farming.

One of the mysteries of railway politics has been the closure of the Cockermouth, Keswick and Penrith branch. The only rail communication with the Lake District is the branch from Oxenholme to Windermere. Northern Lakeland, which contains the finest scenery in England can only be reached by road and during the summer months the roads are clogged with traffic, a situation which gets worse every year. The opening of the M6 Motorway, brings the industrial Midlands within a few hours driving from Keswick, a small town which is virtually the heart of the Lake District. And as the traffic crawls nose to tail from the east towards Keswick, there is the site of the old railway line, with the track lifted and many of the bridges demolished.

Carlisle is not the exciting place it was in pre-grouping days; when the North Eastern worked in from Newcastle, the London and North western from Crewe and places further south; the Glasgow and South Western from Glasgow St Enoch; the Caledonian from Glasgow Central, the North British from Edinburgh, the Midland from St Pancras, and engines from the Maryport and Carlisle Railway pottered around the station.

But even if the colour and the variety have gone, Carlisle is a station with a Border atmosphere. It is the gateway to Scotland or England, depending upon your origins and the direction in which you are travelling. Today, anonymous electrics slide in and out of the station but only ten years ago, you could see a goodly array of Pacifics, A1s, A2s and A3s, from the Waverley Route, and even the occasional A4. There would be "Princess" and "Duchess" pacifics from Euston and Birmingham, "Britannias" and "Clans" from almost anywhere, and "Jubilees" and re-built "Scots" galore. Mid-day and tea time were the busiest times. There was a lot of engine-changing in Citadel station — and all pretty nippy too. Yes, in the days of steam it was a wonderful place to be.

There were sheds at Upperby, Kingmoor, and Canal; once upon a time the Midland had a shed at Durran Hill. The non-stop Royal Scot used to halt briefly at Kingmoor (down) and Upperby (up) to change enginemen. Between Carlisle and the Border of Gretna is the vast new marshalling yard at Kingmoor, which, to me, appears to be larger than it needs to be.

Now, gone are the old signal boxes, no more the dark stains in the sky which identified Kingmoor and Upperby sheds. Carlisle is just an incident on the Inter-City which enables the modern executive to get from Glasgow to London and back within the day, provided he doesn't spend too much time in London!

Below: Pair of English-Electric class 50 diesel-electric locomotives at Carlisle Citadel. D404 from the South hands over to D408 which will take the train on to Glasgow.

Right: Stanier Pacific No 46240 *City of Coventry* in Carlisle Citadel with Glasgow to Birmingham train

Below right: A3 Pacific No 60096 *Papyrus* in Carlisle Citadel with Carlisle to Newcastle train.

Below: Diesel Multiple Unit at Threlkeld with train from Keswick to Carlisle.

Right and below right: Kingmoor Motive Power Depot, after and before dieselisation.

Left: Jubilee 3 cyl 4-6-0
No 45617 *Mauritius* leaves
Carlisle with Birmingham to
Edinburgh train.

53

Above: No 9 *River Mite* leaves Ravenglass with well filled train for Boot

Right: *River Mite* on the turntable at Ravenglass.

Far right: Ravenglass and Eskdale Railway. No 9 *River Mite* near Irton road with train for Boot.

Right: Stanier Pacific
No 46254 *City of Stoke on Trent* leaves Carlisle with up "Royal Scot".

Above: Down "Royal Scot" at Etterby with nearly empty tender. Stanier Pacific No 46242 *City of Glasgow*

Left: Stanier Pacific No 46256 *Sir William Stanier FRS* leaves Carlisle with Birmingham to Glasgow train.

Far left: English Electric type 4 Diesel-Electric passes Kingmoor Shed with down "Royal Scot".

Far left below: Type 45 Sulzer diesel-electric locomotive at Etterby with the down "Thames-Clyde" express.

Above: Stanier Pacific
No 46220 *Coronation,*
streamline casing removed,
leaves Carlisle with down
"Royal Scot".

Above right: "Britannia"
Pacific No 70050 *Firth of
Clyde* at Wreay with Glasgow
to Liverpool and Manchester
train.

Right: Leeds to Glasgow train
approaches Carlisle. Jubilee
3 cyl 4-6-0 No 45589
Gwalior.

Above: Stanier Pacific No 46225 *Duchess of Gloucester* passes Floriston woods with up Mid-day Scot.

Right: Class 8P 4-6-2 *Duke of Gloucester* at Kingmoor with Birmingham to Glasgow train.

THE BORDER: DUMFRIES-SHIRE

Railway-wise, Dumfries-shire possesses two magnificent lines. There is the old Glasgow and South Western line through the Nith Valley — where river, road and railway accompany each other between Dumfries and Kilmarnock.

Dumfries, apart from its attractions as the county town, possesses a well kept station, from which the boat trains ventured forth for Stranraer, and what apocryphal happenings took place on that line as recorded so vividly by Mr David L. Smith. Dumfries shed adjoined the station and its interesting variety of antiques was well viewed from the road to Carlisle.

But the real excitement of this county is the old Caledonian route to Glasgow up and over Beattock. In the ten miles from Beattock station to Summit Box the railway climbs over 1000 feet. Fortunately, trains could get a good run at the bank, and they needed it; bankers were always available at Beattock station, but most drivers of fast passenger trains spurned such assistance, though some wished they hadn't as the Bank began to conquer their engines.

By Greskine Box, which was roughly the half way point, engines were beginning to feel the strain; by Harthope they were sometimes beginning to wonder if they would make the top. "Duchesses" could usually manage up to 400 tons unassisted, but this was often too much for "Princesses". I recall one damp afternoon when a "Princess" pacific with 14 behind the tender passed me at Harthope at walking pace — I know this is true because I walked beside it for quite a distance — its exhaust shooting vertically into the sky, wheels slipping on the damp rail, the fireman shovelling as fast as he could; the cut-off must have been set at 45 to 50%. A wonderful sight and noise indeed, but anxious moments on the footplate.

What a magnificent piece of engineering by Joseph Locke this line is. Soon after leaving Beattock the railway threads the glen of Evan Water and the hills begin to close in. Past Auchencastle, Longbedholm, Greskine, to the Summit, and then with the battle o'er, the train coasts down to Carstairs, where trains for Glasgow and Edinburgh take their separate ways.

On my visits to Beattock I used to stay in Moffat, as pretty a little town as you could wish, well placed too, for exploring the superb Border country and from Moffat it was but a short hop to the railway. In particular I recall one photographic expedition. It was one of those days when the clouds were so low that the hills were invisible, it had rained from sunrise and gave no sign of stopping: came the afternoon when the north-bound procession was due up Beattock — still the rain poured down. After a day stuck in the hotel, for need of something better to do, I took myself off to Harthope to stand in the wet and see what was happening. Almost against my better judgement I went to my favourite spot on the bend at Harthope, and then, to my astonishment, as the "Royal Scot" came into view, the rain stopped, the clouds broke, and for no more than half a minute the sun broke through and I got a magnificent photograph. Then the rain started again, and precisely the same thing happened again when a "Princess" appeared round the bend with the "Birmingham Scot". Such a thing has happened only this once to me. Always it has been the reverse!

Left: Up "Royal Scot" stops at Beattock Summit to take water. Stanier Pacific No 46230 *Duchess of Buccleuch*

Above: Down "Royal Scot" at Harthope, Beattock. Stanier Pacific No 46223 *Princess Alice.*

Right: Up "Royal Scot" nears Elvanfoot. Stanier Pacific No 46224 *Princess Alexandra.*

Left: Re-built Scot No 46157
Royal Artilleryman at
Harthope with Birmingham to
Edinburgh train.

Above: English Electric Class
50 diesel-electric locomotive
No 406 at Greskine with
down "Royal Scot"

Above: London to Perth train at Longbedholm. Jubilee 3 cyl 4-6-0 No 45689 *Ajax*.

Left: Glasgow to Birmingham train at Crawford. Stanier Pacific No 46524 *City of Stoke-on-Trent*.

Far left: Sulzer type 45 English Electric locomotive with the down "Thames-Clyde" express, leaving Dumfries.

Far left below: Pair of English Electric Class 50 diesel-electric locomotives with down "Royal Scot", approaching Dumfries.

Above left: First day of
electric working from
Glasgow to Crewe. Electric
locomotive at Beattock with
southbound train from
Glasgow.

Left: Euston to Perth train at
Harthope. "Jubilee" 3 cyl
4-6-0 No 45640 Frobisher.

Above: "Black 5" No 44796
at Greskine with down Perth
train.

Right: Summer's afternoon at Dumfries: Brush type 47 diesel-electric locomotive No 1675 *Amazon* with train from Perth.

Fire Sale

Only solid fuel offers
summer discounts

1M29

Above: Birmingham to Glasgow train at Longbedholm. "Princess" Pacific No 46210 *Lady Patricia*.

Above right: English Electric type 3 diesel electric approaches Beattock Summit with limestone train.

Right: Down "Caledonian" crosses the Clyde at Crawford. Stanier Pacific No 46232 *Duchess of Montrose*.

Above: Electric locomotive passes Beattock station with express for Glasgow.

Right: "Coronation" Pacific No 46224 *Princess Alexandra* at Harthope with the down "Royal Scot".

Far right: Stanier 2 cyl 4-6-0 No 45721 on the climb to Beattock Summit with afternoon freight train.

Right: "Princess" Pacific No 46209 *Princess Beatrice* blasts its way to Beattock Summit with the Birmingham Scotsman.

Above: Austerity 2-10-0
No 90760 at Harthope with
freight train.

Above right: Up "Thames-
Clyde" express leaves
Dumfries "Jubilee" 3 cyl
4-6-0 No 45657 *Tyrwhitt*.

Right: Pacific No 46223
Princess Alice passes
Beattock station. Two "Black
5s" wait in the station loops
with freight trains.

Above: Electric locomotive E3010 drifts down the bank towards Beattock station with freight train.

Right: Freight leaves Beattock yard for Summit with freight train. Stanier 2 cyl 4-6-0 No 45123

NORTH OF THE BORDER: MIDLOTHIAN

There are some places that after a time one gets used to. The initial magic wears off: the first enchantment fades. Edinburgh is not one of those places, at least, not for me. It is a city with the power to exert its spell anew every time I go there. Dominated by King Arthur's seat and Salisbury Crags with the Palace of Holyrood at the end of the Royal Mile which climbs past Canongate Tolbooth, John Knox's House and St Giles, to the Castle perched on its rock, the city possesses a character unique amongst the cities of Britain. It is every inch a capital city, and knows it. Princes Street, feature by feature is awful, but seen as a whole is magnificent. From end to end it is a collection of shop fronts, many of them belonging to multiple stores; it is a jumble of architectural styles.

On its southward aspect are the Prince's Gardens, where one can play clock golf, listen to the band, buy ice cream, or study the floral clock, but for those who dote on railways, there is the superb view of the line leaving the far end of Waverley Station and heading westward. There are no less than three excellently placed footbridges in the Gardens on which to stand to your hearts content and watch the trains go by. There are many in Edinburgh who could dispute that this is a superb view. They would say that the coming of the railway through Princes Gardens was a monstrous invasion of a place of sylvan charm, and that the greatest disaster of all was the building of Waverley Station between the old town and the new.

I suppose the 19th century conservationists have a point. Viewed from the heights of Princes Gardens, Waverley Station is a horror, but, in the days of steam, it was a place of infinite pleasure to the haunter of stations. It is, basically, one huge island platform with inlet bays at the east and west ends.

In the days when British Railways bestowed names on their trains, a succession of expresses left Waverley bearing such names as "Flying Scotsman", "Elizabethan", "Talisman", "Heart of Midlothian", "Waverley", and "Aberdonian". There was romance about these names, and their departures and arrivals were as much part of Edinburgh life as the march of the Edinburgh Police Band along Princes Street during the Festival.

The locomotives from Haymarket shed were always a joy to behold, because they must have been the cleanest engines in Britain. They reported for duty in Edinburgh Waverley gleaming in every part. The only dirty engines in Edinburgh were those with shed plates indicating that they came from scruffy places south of the Border.

If you could afford it, what better than a night in the North British Hotel with a room looking west along Princes Street? Here you could see and hear the trains coming and going from the station below, and if you could not sleep you could always go for a walk in the station, and you might get a cup of tea in the Waverley Station East Box.

To climb Calton Hill late on a summer's evening; to look across the Firth of Forth with Leith sprawling below you; to turn your eye to the west and see the Castle floodlit and apparently suspended in the sky, and to hear the boom of the whistle of an A4 in the station almost under your feet, was an experience never to be forgotten.

Above: Deltic No 9009
Alycidon at Edinburgh
Waverley with the up "Flying
Scotsman".

Above right: A4 Pacific
No 60012 *Commonwealth of
Australia* leaves Calton Tunnel
with Glasgow to Kings Cross
train.

Right: A3 Pacific No 60094
Colorado leaves Edinburgh
Waverley for Glasgow with
the "North Briton".

Above: A4 Pacific No 60024 *Kingfisher* passes Portobello East box with Glasgow-Kings Cross train.

Right: Up "Queen of Scots" Pullman at Portobello East. A3 Pacific No 60090 *Grand Parade*.

Far right above: Up afternoon "Talisman" at Portobello East. "Deltic" 9003 "Meld".

Far right: Edinburgh to Carlisle train at Portobello East. A3 Pacific No 60095 *Flamingo*.

Right: A4 Pacific No 60007
Sir Nigel Gresley leaves
Edinburgh Waverley with
Glasgow to Kings Cross
express.

Above: Two "Deltics" at Haymarket Sheds. 9009 *Alycidon* and 9006 *Fife and Forfar Yeomanry*.

Above right: Diesel-electric power at Haymarket Shed.

Right: Up "Elizabethan" leaves Edinburgh Waverley. A4 Pacific No 60024 *Kingfisher*.

Above left: "Deltic" No 9013
Black Watch and Brush
type 47 No D1976 at
Haymarket.

Left: A2 Pacific No 60535
Hornet's Beauty in Princes
Street Gardens with train for
Aberdeen.

Above: Two Birmingham
RCW class 26/0 diesel-
electrics in Princes Street
Gardens with Edinburgh to
Aberdeen train.

Above: Up afternoon
"Talisman" emerges from
Calton Tunnel. "Deltic"
No 9018 *Ballymoss*.

Right: Afternoon train from
Edinburgh to Aberdeen in the
Princes Street Gardens. Brush
type 47 diesel-electric
No 1969.

Far right: Glasgow to London
train at Portobello East. A4
Pacific No 60012
Commonwealth of Australia.

Above: Standard Class 5
4-6-0 No 73152
crosses the Forth Bridge with
train from Dundee.

Above left: Morning
"Talisman" leaves Edinburgh
Waverley.

Left: Afternoon "Talisman"
leaves Edinburgh Waverley.
"Deltic" No 9009 *Alycidan*.

Above: "Deltic" 9021 *Argyll and Sutherland Highlander* waits for the off in Edinburgh Waverley with the up "Elizabethan".

Above: A1 Pacific No 60161
North British leaves
Edinburgh Waverley with the
up "Queen of Scots".

THE NORTH EAST

Northumberland is the least discovered of the beautiful counties in the North. To the South, the coast line is heavily industrial with coal mining as the principal industry, but north of Warkworth, the coast is superb. Inland, are the Cheviots; not dramatic hills but rolling and rounded, and at Kirk Yetholm is the northern terminus of the Pennine Way.

The railway has a fairly easy time of it; there is nothing much to extend a locomotive, although there is some hard work to be done north of the Border at Cockburnspath — at least there *was* in the days of steam.

Berwick-on-Tweed is not the actual border, as many think it to be; the border is actually at Marshall's Meadows, an undistinguished caravan site about 3 miles north of Berwick.

The town has a ruined castle from which a splendid view of the railway can be obtained as it comes round Stephenson's magnificent viaduct spanning the Tweed. There are three bridges at Berwick. Nearest the sea there is the old road bridge, next, there is the new road bridge, and then the railway viaduct. Berwick is a place with atmosphere. It is a walled town, as I realised when we stayed in a small hotel by the walls from which curious pedestrians could look straight in to our bedroom, and could almost take the soap of the wash stand.

Left: Down "Capitals Express" at Alnmouth. A4 Pacific No 60022 *Mallard*.

Far left: Edinburgh to Aberdeen express leaving Waverley behind A1 Pacific No 60162.

Right: Glasgow to London train at Cockburnspath. Brush type 47 diesel-electric D1786.

Below right: Newcastle to Edinburgh train descends the bank at Cockburnspath. English Electric type 4 diesel-electric No 259.

Below: A4 Pacific No 60024 *Kingfisher* at Grantshouse with the down "Elizabethan".

Right: Down "Flying Scotsman" at Newcastle. A4 Pacific No 60009 *Union of South Africa*.

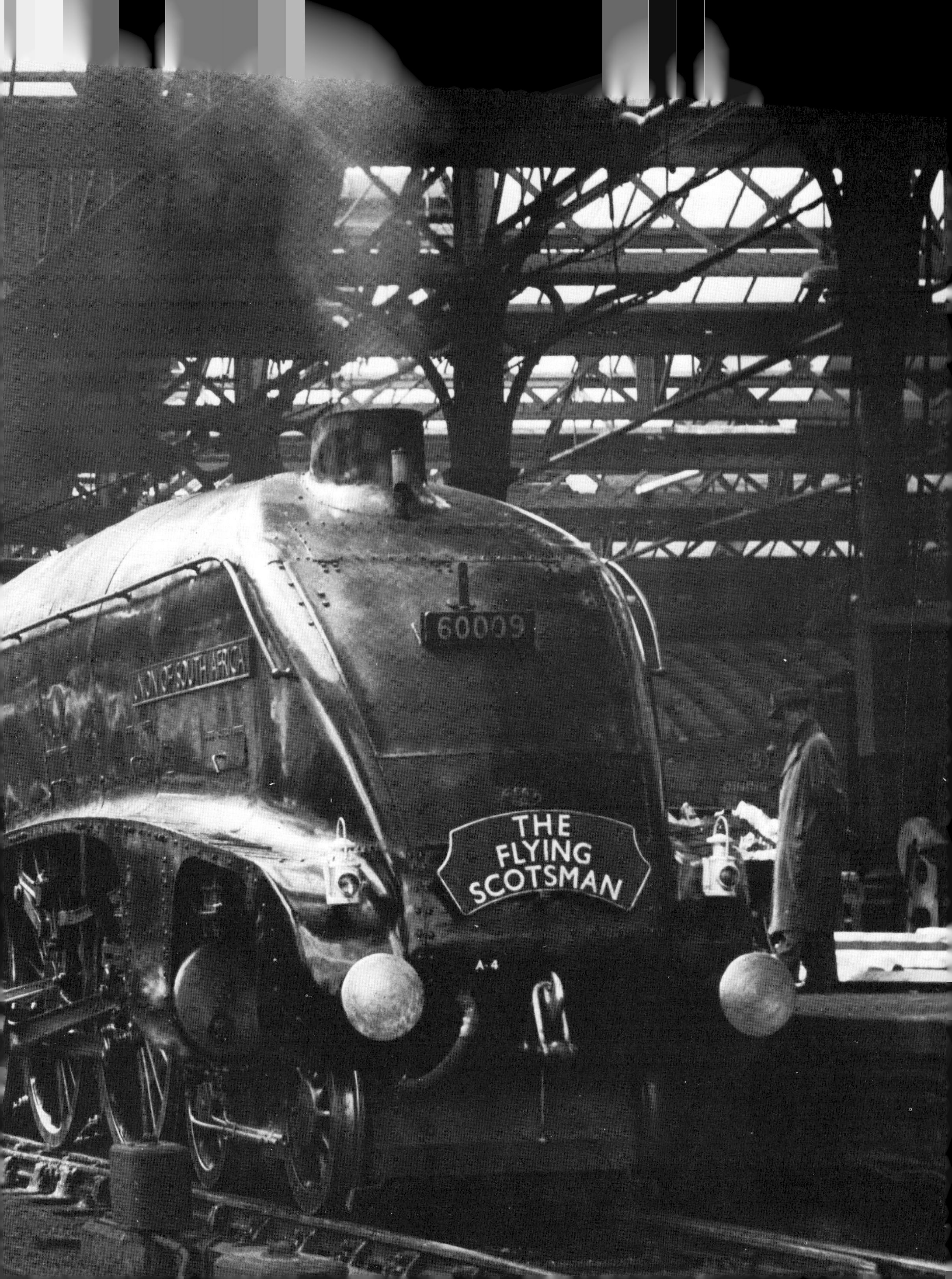
60009
UNION OF SOUTH AFRICA
THE FLYING SCOTSMAN
A 4
DINING

Above: Crossing the Border: A3 Pacific No 60071 *Tranquil* passes the Border signs at Marshall Meadows with London to Edinburgh Express.

Left: Down "Flying Scotsman" leaves Newcastle Central. A4 Pacific No 60011 *Empire of India*.

Far left above: London to Edinburgh train leaves Berwick-on-Tweed. "Deltic" No 9021 *Argyll and Sutherland Highlander*.

Far left below: "Deltic"-hauled Scottish Express crosses the Royal Border Bridge at Berwick-on-Tweed.

Above: A4 Pacific No 60007
Sir Nigel Gresley leaves
Newcastle Central with
Edinburgh to London train.

FURTHER NORTH

This rather vague title describes journeys north of Edinburgh and south of a line from Inverness to the Kyle of Lochalsh. It will always be a matter of regret to me that I did not venture into these northern regions in the days of steam, except for the west coast, in the area of Fort William and the Kyle.

The railway from Inverness to the Kyle of Lochalsh is incomparably the most beautiful in the British Isles. From Achnasheen it threads glens of unsurpassed splendour. If you are sound in wind and limb it is worth alighting at Achnashellach and taking the mountain path to Glen Torridon; ten miles of hard slog rewarded by superb views of Ben Eighe and Liathach. After the return journey of twenty miles, you will be very glad to get back into the train, but you may have to wait a long time for it, as there are only two a day each way.

The climax of the journey is from Strathcarron station to the Kyle. The line is perched on the rocky hillside above the waters of Loch Carron. Across the loch are the superb hills of Applecross, then as the line turns southward there are the Coulins on the Isle of Skye. Kyle station is alongside the quayside, and a half a mile across the narrows is Kyleakin on Skye. Praise the Lord, the closure of this magnificent piece of railway has been postponed, for apart from its tourist attraction, it is clearly a social necessity to those who live in this remote corner of Scotland. In the latter years of steam it was worked entirely by Black 5's; type 2 Diesel Electrics now do the job competently but with less dramatic impact.

The Mallaig extension from Fort William is another "must" for the enthusiastic traveller. The old West Highland traverses the shores of Loch Eil with magnificent views of Ben Nevis from Corpach until it crosses the Glenfinnan Viaduct from which Loch Shiel can be seen stretching away to the south. Then along Loch Ailort to Arisaig. Away across the silvery sands and the blue sea are the islands of Rhum and Eigg and the mountains of Skye, and so into Mallaig with its pervading smell of fish and the squalling of scavenging gulls.

Below: Type 4 English Electric No D340 leaves Inverness with train for London Kings Cross.

Above: Two class 25 Diesel-
Electrics at Inverness on the
"Royal 'Highlander".

Above: K2 2-6-0 No 61687
Loch Quoich at Fort William
with morning train for Mallaig.

Above: K2 2-6-0 No 61788
Loch Rannoch making up its
train in the goods yard at Fort
William.

Right: Class 26/1 BRC&W
diesel-electric No 5336 at
Kyle of Lochalsh on evening
train to Inverness.

Colour Section
Far right: On the North
Yorkshire Moors Line. Ex
N.C.B. 0-6-2T No 29 at
Beckfoot.

Above: K2s No 61787 *Loch Quoich* and No 61788 *Loch Rannoch* leave Fort William with train for Glasgow.

Right: No 5336 (Class 26/1) leaves Kyle of Lochalsh for Inverness.

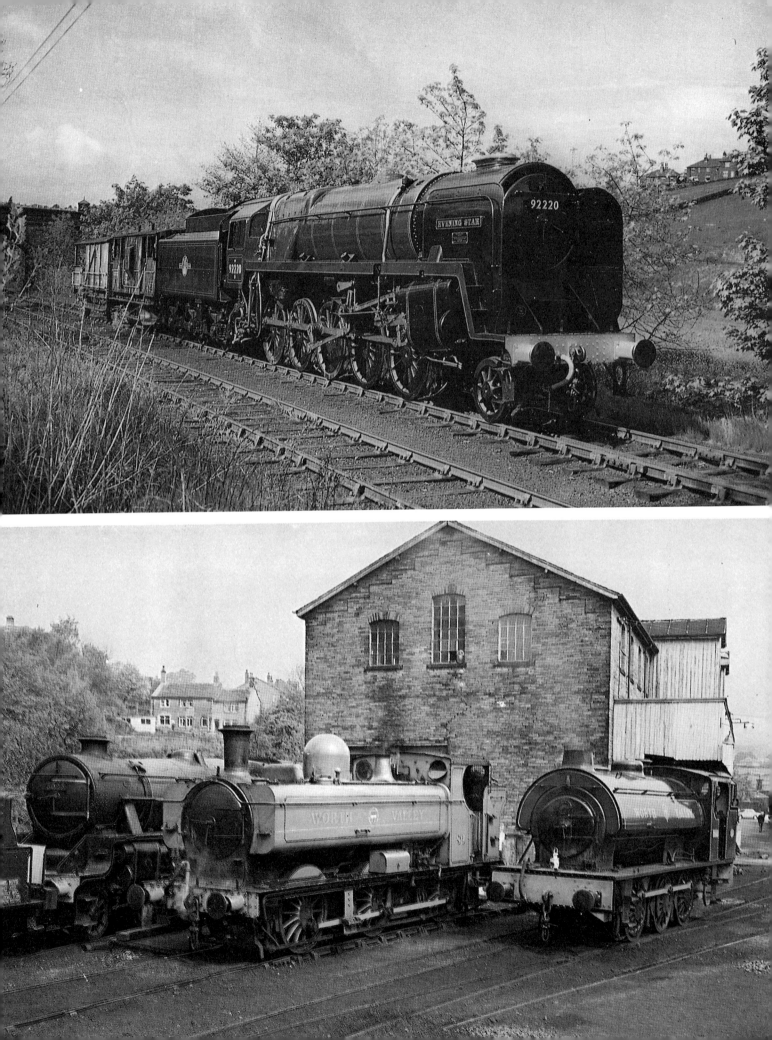

Above: Class 26/1 diesel-electric approaches Lairg with morning train for Thurso.

Left: Pair of Type 2 Beyer Peacock diesel-electrics at Aviemore with train for Inverness.

Colour Section
Opposite page top: B.R. 2-10-0 No 92220 *Evening Star* photographed on the day of its arrival at Haworth for working on the Keighley and Worth Valley Railway.

Opposite page bottom: Scene in the yard at Haworth. Left to right Stanier 2cyl 4-6-0 No 5212, ex London Transport 0-6-0 Pannier Tank No L89, and ex N.C.B. 0-6-0 *Fred*.

Below: Type 2 diesel-electric leaves Inverness with morning train for Kyle of Lochalsh.

Left: Type 2 diesel-electric stopping at Achnasheen with Inverness-Kyle of Lochalsh train.

Below left: Type 2 Beyer Peacock diesel-electric leaves Inverness with morning train to Thurso.

COUNTY OF YORK NORTH YORKSHIRE

The Local Government re-organisers have decreed that there be three Yorkshires — West, North and South, but to every true Yorkshireman, born or adopted, there will only be one Yorkshire. And there will only be one Yorkshire in the County Cricket Championship.

The new North Yorkshire County Area has, as its County town, Northallerton, though why the City of York was overlooked for this honour is difficult to understand. From Selby to Tee-side runs the main line from Kings Cross.

Across the swing bridge at Selby, over the level crossings at Riccall, skirting the archi-episcopal village of Bishopthorpe, the train runs into York station. A beautiful spacious station built on a curve, with a magnificent cast iron all-over vaulting which follows the curve round. In the days of steam it used to be a thing to hear and see as an A3 Pacific tried to re-start a heavy train stopped on the curve.

Then past the locomotive yards, away across the Plain of York to Darlington. It was somewhere along here, Pilmoor, I think, where engine crews used to change on the non-stops from Edinburgh to London. On the up run, the Kings Cross men would leave the "cushions" and edge through the tender corridor and take over from the Haymarket crew, who would take it easy to Kings Cross, and vice versa on the down run.

Between Darlington and Newcastle there is to be seen one of the most superb views in the British Isles. As the train crosses the viaduct approaching Durham station, the Cathedral towers over the roofs of the city, a view preferably seen on an autumn morning, as that great Cathedral stands silhouetted against the eastern sky, rising out of the smoky mists of Durham. A view which is the very epitome of the North — this great building which is the last resting place of the bones of Cuthbert, that great northern saint.

If you are a haunter of preserved lines, you must take yourself in an easterly direction to visit the North Yorkshire Moors Railway which is steam operated from Grosmont to Goathland.

The journey from York by road takes you through Malton and Pickering, two attractive market towns. After Pickering you come out on to the North Yorkshire moors, which are breath-takingly beautiful, especially in late summer when the heather is blooming. Down in the valley of Newtondale you can see the line winding up the hill to Pickering, then you will see what appear to be three enormous golf balls nestling in the heather. This is the "Early Warning" station at Fylingdale, and beyond, the North Sea.

Then down the hill to Grosmont, where, in the summer, there will be a lot happening in the station, as trains are prepared for the day's work. You might even see a Black 5 No 5428 bearing the name *Eric Treacy*. Soon after this engine's arrival at Grosmont, it was my pleasure to celebrate my birthday by taking charge of the engine for a morning's duty up and down the bank to Goathland. Somehow the news of my turn on the engine leaked out, with the result that a surprising number of the faithful from the Diocese of Wakefield found themselves on the Moors that morning in order to cheer their bishop on.

Above: Up "Flying Scotsman" approaches York station. "Deltic" No 9011 *Royal Northumberland Fusiliers*.

Right: London to Newcastle train leaves York. A3 Pacific No 60077 *White Knight*.

Above: Train for Edinburgh
and Glasgow in York station.
"Deltic" No 9000 *Royal
Scots Greys.*

Above: York to Bristol train at
Holgate, York. "Jubilee" 3 cyl
4-6-0 No 45662 *Kempenfelt*.

Above: Up "Flying Scotsman"
passes through York station.
"Deltic" No 9013 *The Black
Watch*.

Above: NYMR Another pair at Grosmont. Two ex-Lambton 0-6-2s No 5 and No 29.

Right: NYMR. Scene at Grosmont Shed. Stanier Class 5 4-6-0 No 5428 *Eric Treacy* and ex-Lambton 0-6-2T No 5.

Far right: North Yorkshire Moors Railway. Ex-Lambton 0-6-2 No 29 brewing up at Grosmont.

Above: Class J72 0-6-0T, although with express headlamps, shunts mixed stock at York.

Right: Kings Cross to Glasgow train at Challoner's Whin, York. "Deltic" No 9006 *Fife and Forfar Yeomanry*.

Above: Up "Heart of Midlothian" leaves York. A1 Pacific No 60144 *King's Courier*.

Above: Newcastle train leaves York. A2 Pacific 60526 *Sugar Palm*.

Above right: V2 2-6-2 at Northallerton with train from East Anglia to Newcastle.

Right: A2 Pacific 60526 *Sugar Palm* with the up "Queen of Scots" passes B1 4-6-0 No 61254 heading a freight train on the approaches to Northallerton.

Left: NYMR. Stanier Class 5
4-6-0 No 5428 *Eric Treacy*
at Beck Hole with a train for
Goathland.

Colour Section

Above: Scene at North End of
Steamtown, Carnforth. In
centre Gresley's V2 2-6-2
Green Arrow and A4 Pacific
Sir Nigel Gresley

Above: Brush type 47 diesel-
electric No 1991 leaves York
with a train for Newcastle.

134

Above: A3 Pacific No 60103
Flying Scotsman at Holgate
with Newcastle to Kings
Cross train.

Above: NYMR. P3 0-6-0
No 2392 goes for the summit
south of Goathland.

Left: NYMR. Ex-Lambton
0-6-2 No 29 between Beck
Hole and Goathland.

Colour Section
Far left: Ivatt 2-6-2 tank No
41241 approaches Oxenhope
with afternoon train from
Keighley.

Above left, left and above:
York Motive Power Depot.

Above: Up "Tees-Tyne Pullman" at Dringhouses. A4 Pacific No 60022 *Mallard*.

Right: "Deltic" No 9014 *Duke of Wellington's Regiment* leaves York for the north with Scottish express.

Above right: Brush type 47 diesel-electric No 1576 rounds the curve at Challoner's Whin with up Newcastle express.

140

Right: Brush Type 47 diesel-electric waits at platform 9 in York station with train for Newcastle.

Below right: "Deltic" No 9016 *Gordon Highlander* in York station with the down "Flying Scotsman."

Below: Up "Flying Scotsman" threads York Station. "Deltic" No 9019 *Royal Highland Fusilier.*

Above: Down morning "Talisman" halts in York station. Sulzer type 45 diesel-electric (left) with train from Sheffield.

Right: Diesel maintenance shop at York.

THE 'LONG DRAG'

Anyone who has travelled on the footplate of a steam locomotive from Settle to Blea Moor will appreciate how this wonderful bit of railway earned this name. I have travelled on the footplates of "Jubilees", re-built "Scots", "Britannias", and A3 pacifics up the hill from Settle, and, verily, it is a long drag. Ten miles at 1 in 90, often with violent cross winds and wet rails.

It is a magnificent line, albeit expensive to maintain, in view of its tunnels and bridges. From Leeds, there is not much to be said for it — just rather drab West Riding industry. After Skipton, the landscape begins to improve as the train enters the Craven Country. Away to the west is Pendle Hill. Through Hellifield, its days past as a northern railway centre: above the roofs of Settle, and then the work used to start, as the train hit the bottom of the bank. Regulator fully open, cut off back to 30% or 35%, and an increase in noise from the locomotive front end. The shovel was used "more and often", as the train threaded one of the wildest dales in Yorkshire. Ribblesdale is lime-stone grit, sheep, pot holes and running water of which the presiding monarchs are Ingleborough, Whernside, and Pen-y-Ghent. Past the Ribblehead viaduct, our labouring engine would plunge into the long wet Blea Moor Tunnel, and then out into a new world. Here the line is perched on the hill side, and to the west is the green pastoral dale of Dent. All labour over, it would now coast along the level to Ais Gill, having replenished its water supply on the Garsdale troughs, the highest in England. From Ais Gill it is downhill to Appleby.

From Ais Gill to Kirkby Stephen, the scenery is superb. To the west, Wild Boar Fell broods over the line; to the east, the high Mallerstang Common. Down the hill the engine dashes with but a breath of steam.

Appleby past, along the Eden Valley; between the hills of Cumberland, and the Pennine Ridge — Cross Fell and Dufton Pike, and the beautiful red soil of this superb valley. And so to Carlisle.

The rugged re-built "Scots" seemed just right in this country, but I have to admit that Gresley's A3 Pacifics, during their short spell on this line were the least disturbed by the demands made on them. They just walked up the hill!

It would be a sad thing should this line ever be closed. We salute the enginemen who have tackled the "Long Drag" in all weathers, and their firemen who have shifted numberless tons of coal up the hill.

Below: "Jubilee" 4-6-0 No 45691 *Orion* on freight train at Ribblehead.

Above: Northbound freight
train at Ais Gill. Class 4F
0-6-0 No 4482.

Above: English Electric Type 4 diesel-electric D236 at Ais Gill with train of limestone.

Left: Type 2 Beyer Peackock diesel-electric No 5190 leaves the goods loop at Ais Gill with southbound freight.

Above: Local train leaves Rise
Hill tunnel and approaches
Dent. 2-6-4T No 42484.

Right: Class 4F 0-6-0
No 4404 at Kildwick with
freight train.

Above: Class 8F 2-8-0
No 48443 with freight train at
Garsdale water troughs, the
highest in England.

Right: Northbound freight
train at Helwith Bridge. Class
4F 0-6-0 and class 8F 2-8-0.

Above: Down "Waverley Express" at Marley Junction, near Keighley. Standard Class 5 4-6-0 No 73166.

Above right: Down "Thames-Clyde Express" at Dent. Sulzer Type 45 diesel-electric D85.

Right: Northbound freight train crosses the River Ribble near Stainforth. Stanier 2 cyl Class 5 4-6-0.

Right: Re-built "Scot"
No 46145 *Duke of
Wellington's Regiment* leaves
Leed City with down
"Thames-Clyde Express"

152

Right: Freight train at Ais Gill
Sulzer type 45 diesel-electric.

Below: Northbound freight
train at Horton in Ribblesdale.

COUNTY OF YORK
WEST YORKSHIRE

If you were to say that there is a disproportionate number of photographs in this book from the old West Riding, you would be right! There are, because this is my home patch.

The lines into and out of Leeds, presented a rich variety of steam motive power. Holbeck Shed in its latter days, gave shelter to Gresley A3 Pacifics, occasionally an A1, Britannia Pacifics, rebuilt Scots, Jubilees, and numerous Black 5s. Copley Hill had a stud of beautifully clean A1s and A3s.

Central Station was a poky place with the great disadvantage that trains, immediately on leaving the station, hit the bottom of a gradient which extended for a mile and a half, as far as Wortley South Box. Originally the old G.N. station, it specialised in trains to Doncaster, Kings Cross and Edinburgh, thus there was a procession of Gresley and Peppercorn Pacifics. A couple of hundred yards up the hill, at the old Holbeck station, the G.N. line passed over the Midland line on its way to Glasgow and the Lancashire coast. Now Central Station is no more. Leeds City station was always a place of interest; from the west end, the old Midland and LNWR lines departed, respectively, for St Pancras, Glasgow, and lesser places in between, and for Liverpool and Manchester, threading the Pennines at Standedge Tunnel. From the east end of the station, trains departed for Hull, York, Newcastle and for many years my official duties took me frequently from Halifax to Wakefield, and with careful planning I could so arrange my route that I could nip out of the car, and in a couple of minutes catch the 9·50am train from Leeds to Kings Cross. Between morning and afternoon meetings, I took my sandwiches from Wakefield to Leeds, and spent my lunch hour, in Leeds A Box or Holbeck Shed.

The Committee room in Church House, Wakefield, looked out on the viaduct over which the London trains to and from Leeds passed, and under which the old L&Y lines headed east and west. Thus it was, that ecclesiastical committee meetings were not as dull as they might have been, although there was from time to time, a certain lack of concentration on the part of the then Archdeacon of Halifax. It was not so easy when I was Chairman of a Committee and some ticklish point of procedure was being argued as the up "White Rose" was crossing the viaduct behind an A3! Actually, I was not the only one in the room with an eye not focussed on the agenda! It is curious how many men of the Cloth share this peculiar interest in the Steam Engine. I am often asked why this is, and I have to plead ignorance. It could be that it is the attraction of opposites; the parson is, ideally, a man of peace and the controlled violence of steam expresses the aggression he often feels but has to keep in check.

In any account of railways in the ex-West Riding, mention must be made of the Worth Valley Railway. Now ten years old and in good nick. Five miles of standard gauge railway from Keighley to Oxenhope. I doubt if any preserved line can produce such a variety of motive power in a season, including *Evening Star**, a Black 5, a W.D. 2-8-0 rescued from the Arctic Circle, a Fairburn and an Ivatt 2-6-4 tank, a number of ex-industrial tank engines and a 4F 0-6-0, and before long, one of the Bulleid "West Country" Pacifics will be "chuffing" up the hill.

*Now departed for the York Railway Museum

Above: Up "Thames Clyde Express" leaves Leeds City Station. BR Standard class 5 4-6-0 No 73010 pilots "Jubilee" 3 cyl 4-6-0 No 45694 *Bellerophon*.

Right: A3 Pacific No 60036 "*Colombo*" on the "North Briton" in Leeds City Station.

Above: V2 2-6-2 No 60982
at Holbeck with the down
"Queen of Scots" Pullman.

Above: Keighley and Worth
Valley Railway. Train on
Mytholmes Viaduct. J94
0-6-0 No 68077 *Fred* pilots
Class 5 4-6-0 No 5025.

Deltics at Wakefield:

Left: 9004 *Queens Own Highlander* passes Lofthouse Colliery with up "Queen of Scots".

Below left: 9000 *Royal Scots Greys* approaches Wakefield. Westgate with up "Queen of Scots".

Below: 9003 *Meld* at Wakefield Westgate with London train. The clock tower has now been demolished.

Above: Leeds Central to London train at Copley Hill. A3 Pacific No 60066 *Merry Hampton.*

Above: Deltic No 9015 *Tulyar*
marshals London train at
Leeds Central.

Above: A3 Pacific No 60044 *Melton* at Beeston with train for Doncaster and East Anglia.

Above: B1 4-6-0 No 61218 leaves Leeds City with train for Scarborough.

Left: A3 Pacific No 60110 *Robert the Devil* at Copley Hill, Leeds with evening train for London.

Below: Class 9F 2-10-0
No 92220 *Evening Star*, on
loan to the Keighley and
Worth Valley Railway crosses
the Mytholmes Viaduct en
route for Oxenhope.

Right: *Kestrel* at Sandal with
the up "Yorkshire Pullman".

Below right: Sulzer Type 45
diesel-electric at Beeston
with the up "Yorkshire
Pullman".

Right: The "North Briton" in the outskirts of Leeds. A3 Pacific No 60074 *Harvester*.

Above left: Class 4P 3 cyl
Compound pilots Stanier 2 cyl
4-6-0 at Longwood,
Huddersfield with Newcastle
to Liverpool train.

Left: A4 Pacific No 60030
Golden Fleece at Tingley with
morning train from Leeds to Kings
Cross.

Above: B1 4-6-0 No 61387 at
Wortley with East Anglian
train.

Above: A4 No 60022 *Mallard*
at Copley Hill Shed.

Above: Class 9F 2-10-0 *Evening Star* at Ingrow.

Left: "Deltic" No 9007 *Pinza* passes Copley Hill Shed with Leeds to London train.

Above: Newcastle to
Liverpool train leaves Leeds
City. Stanier 2 cyl 4-6-0
No 44684 pilots Rebuilt
"Scot" No 46124 *London
Scottish.*

Above: Northbound "North Briton" sets out for Glasgow from Leeds City Station. A3 Pacific No 60086 *Gainsboro*.

Above: *Evening Star* and *Hamburg* back down to Keighley from Haworth.

Above right: Keighley and Worth Valley Railway. Longmoor Military Railway 0-6-0 Saddle tank *Brussells* pilots Manchester Ship Canal 0-6-0 *Hamburg*.

Right: *Hamburg* and L&Y "Pug" saddle tank in the yards at Haworth.

Above: Class G5 0-4-4T
No 67263 leaves Leeds City
with train for Harrogate.

Above right: A4 Pacific
No 60030 *Golden Fleece* at
Copley Hill with London Kings
Cross train.

Right: A1 Pacific No 60139
Sea Eagle coasts down the
hill from Ardsley with London
train to Leeds. On left, Class
J6 0-6-0 No 64277.

Above left: "Yorkshire Pullman" near Lofthouse, Wakefield. Brush Type 47 diesel-electric No 1532.

Left: Westbound freight train at Linthwaite on climb from Huddersfield to Standedge Tunnel. Austerity 2-8-0 No 90732.

Above: Brush Type 47 diesel-electric No 1505 at Ardsley with up "Queen of Scots" Pullman.

Far left: A3 Pacific No 60103 *Flying Scotsman* climbs the bank from Leeds Central to Holbeck with the up "White Rose".

Above: Up "Thames Clyde Express" passes Holbeck Sheds. "Jubilee" 3 cyl 4-6-0 No 45739 *Ulster*.

Left: "Deltic" No 9018, later named *Ballymoss* passes Holbeck station with train from Leeds to London.

Top: Stanier 2 cyl 4-6-0
No 45212 crosses
Mytholmes Viaduct with train
from Keighley to Oxenhope.

Above: Same train enters
Mytholmes Tunnel.

Right: Class 9F No 92220
Evening Star photographed
on the day of its arrival at
Haworth.

Above: Down "Thames-Clyde Express" at Wortley Junction, Leeds. Rebuilt "Scot" 4-6-0 No 46117 *Welsh Guardsman*.

Above: Type 2 Brush diesel-electric No D5836 at Horbury with freight train.

Left: A4 Pacific No 60006 *Sir Ralph Wedgwood* at Wortley South with train from Leeds to London.

Below: *Falcon* adds the Harrogate portion of the "Yorkshire Pullman" to the Leeds cars at Leeds Central.

Right: Sulzer Type 45 diesel-electrics at the refuelling point at Holbeck.

Below right: Holbeck shed: Class 5 2 cyl 4-6-0 No 45428 on the turntable.

Above: Newcastle to
Liverpool train at Gledholt,
Huddersfield. "Patriot" 4-6-0
No 45220 *Llandudno* pilots
Stanier class 5MT.

Right: Class 4MT 2-6-4T
(Fowler) No 42412 leaves
Leeds with stopping train for
Manchester.

Above: Light and shade in
Holbeck shed.

Above: Two "Jubilees" leave
Leeds City at the head of train
from Newcastle to Liverpool.

Above: B1 4-6-0 No 61372 emerges from the roundhouse at Holbeck shed.

Left: Class A2/2 Pacific No 60501 *Cock o' the North* at Wortley Junction with the down "Queen of Scots" Pullman.

COUNTY OF YORK
SOUTH YORKSHIRE

Doncaster is the point at which lines converge from Lincoln and East Anglia, from London and Sheffield; from Hull in the East, from the Far North, and from Leeds, Bradford and the industrial West Riding that was.

Like Crewe it has a long history as a railway town, and the "Plant" provided employment for a high proportion of the citizens of Doncaster. There still remain a large number of railwaymen who were trained at Doncaster, a town which generated a remarkable loyalty — a loyalty which is all the more powerful when it is confronted with similar loyalties to Derby or Crewe.

Doncaster men have great pride in the engines designed and built at Doncaster and they are always ready to speak of the superiority of their machines over those built further West. It was, perhaps, tactless to point out to them that Doncaster never produced a 4-6-0 to equal Stanier's Black 5. They always claim that Gresley's V2's were the engines that won the war! No one will deny the sterling performance of the V2s which kept going through the dark years of the war, very short on maintenance, and filthy externally; they were strong engines which could be flayed by their drivers. Often they were to be seen at the head of twenty coaches during the war years, grunting and clanking, but never giving in!

My first experience of Doncaster was in 1944 when I spent a few nights sleeping in the "tote" on the racecourse. My Regiment was on the way south, down the Great North Road to Tilbury, where we embarked for Normandy. I did not think much of it as a place. I have come to think better of it as I have been allowed to visit the "Plant" and the engine sheds and to meet the "natives".

Doncaster to London is now but two hours travelling time, and for those travelling from the North it is the beginning of the South. As soon as you get to Bawtry, there is the feeling that the hard north is giving way to the gentler south, and almost before you have finished your breakfast and paid your bill, you are pulling into Kings Cross. When the APT is in service, there will scarce be time to eat a decent breakfast!

Above: "Deltic" No 9020 *Nimbus* passes Doncaster with down morning "Talisman".

Right: Kings Cross to Newcastle train approaches Doncaster. Brush type 4 diesel-electric D1506.

CREWE—CHESTER— HOLYHEAD

It might be said that to include Holyhead in the "North" is stretching things a bit far. The same might be said for Crewe which is almost in the Potteries, and whose inhabitants scarcely think of themselves as Northerners. However, as I have one or two photographs that I like which were taken in this area, I plead authors' license.

It is many years now since I visited Holyhead shed, but I recall my visits with the greatest pleasure. Geoffrey Dentith was the shed master, an enthusiast if ever there was one. The re-built "Scots" allocated to the shed for working the "Irish Mails" were kept in superb condition, and the drivers were great co-operators when smoke was needed.

The cuttings and tunnels between Chester and Saltney were rich in photographic possibilities. Here was one of the few places in England where up and down trains were to be found travelling in the same direction. On leaving Chester General, the up Birkenhead-Paddington train travelled alongside the down "Irish Mail" on adjacent tracks.

As for Crewe, what is there to be said about it that has not already been said by those who write on Railways? At the north end the trains come from Holyhead and Chester, from Liverpool and Scotland, from Manchester and industrial Lancashire. At the South end, they come from Stoke, from London and Birmingham, and from Shrewsbury and South Wales. In the days of steam Crewe was a place throbbing with activity: a place of never ending interest to the enthusiast. Today, it is cleaner, but it no longer has the feel of being the heart of a great railway system.

Left: Crewe 1974. Euston train leaves the station with the new motive power.

Above: Manchester to Euston train leaves Crewe Locomotive E3152.

Above right: Two electric locomotives parked in Crewe station.

Right: Rebuilt "Scot" 4-6-0 No 6115 *Scots Guardsman* leaves Chester General with "H and C" train.

On pages 200/1: Western Region "Star" Class 4-6-0 *Knight of Saint Patrick* leaves Chester with train for Shrewsbury.

Above: Western Region
"Castle" class 4-6-0 No 5033
Broughton Castle leaves
Chester with stopping train to
Shrewsbury.

Left: Western Region
"County" Class 4-6-0
No 1016 *County of Hants*
emerges from tunnel through
the walls at Chester with
afternoon train from
Birkenhead to Paddington.

Above: Class 4F 0-6-0
No 44079 threads the walls
at Chester with freight train.

Above: Ex L&Y 0-6-0 3F
No 52119 shunts empty
stock at Bangor.

Above: Holyhead sheds: Left,
Class 4P 3 cyl compound
4-4-0 No 1158. Right, rebuilt
"Scot" 4-6-0 No 46127 *Old
Contemptibles*.

Far left: Class 5MT Stanier 4-6-0 No 44742 fitted with Caprotti valve gear at Llandudno with train for Manchester.

Above: Rebuilt "Scot" 4-6-0 No 46132 *The King's Regiment, Liverpool* leaves Holyhead with "Horse and Carriage".

Left: Train from Llandudno to Bangor at Bethesda Junction. G2 Class 7F 0-8-0 No 49291.

Right: Stanier Pacific
No 46254 *City of Stoke-on-Trent*, front end view.

Above: Stanier Pacific
No 46240 *City of Coventry* at Crewe, after removing of streamline casing.

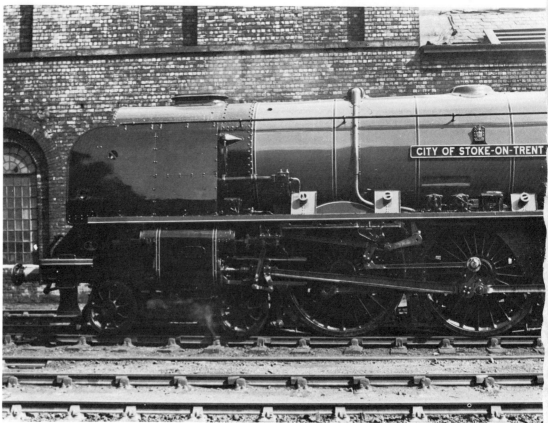